RONDO

(from "Rondo for Violin and Piano," WoO41*)

Ludwig van Beethoven
arr. by Wesley Schaum

* WoO = Without Opus Number

ROMANCE

(from "A Little Night Music," KV525)

Wolfgang A. Mozart
arr. by Wesley Schaum

mp
cresc.
rit.
f
a tempo
mp
f
dim.
rit.
p

CHINESE GONG

Original Solo by
Ladonna Weston

* Pedal is to be depressed on the 2nd beat.

a tempo
p
pp
8va
a tempo
p
cresc.
mf
cresc.
f
basso marcato
rit.
sf
8va

HOW GREAT THOU ART

Words by John W. Schaum

Swedish Folk Melody
arr. by John W. Schaum

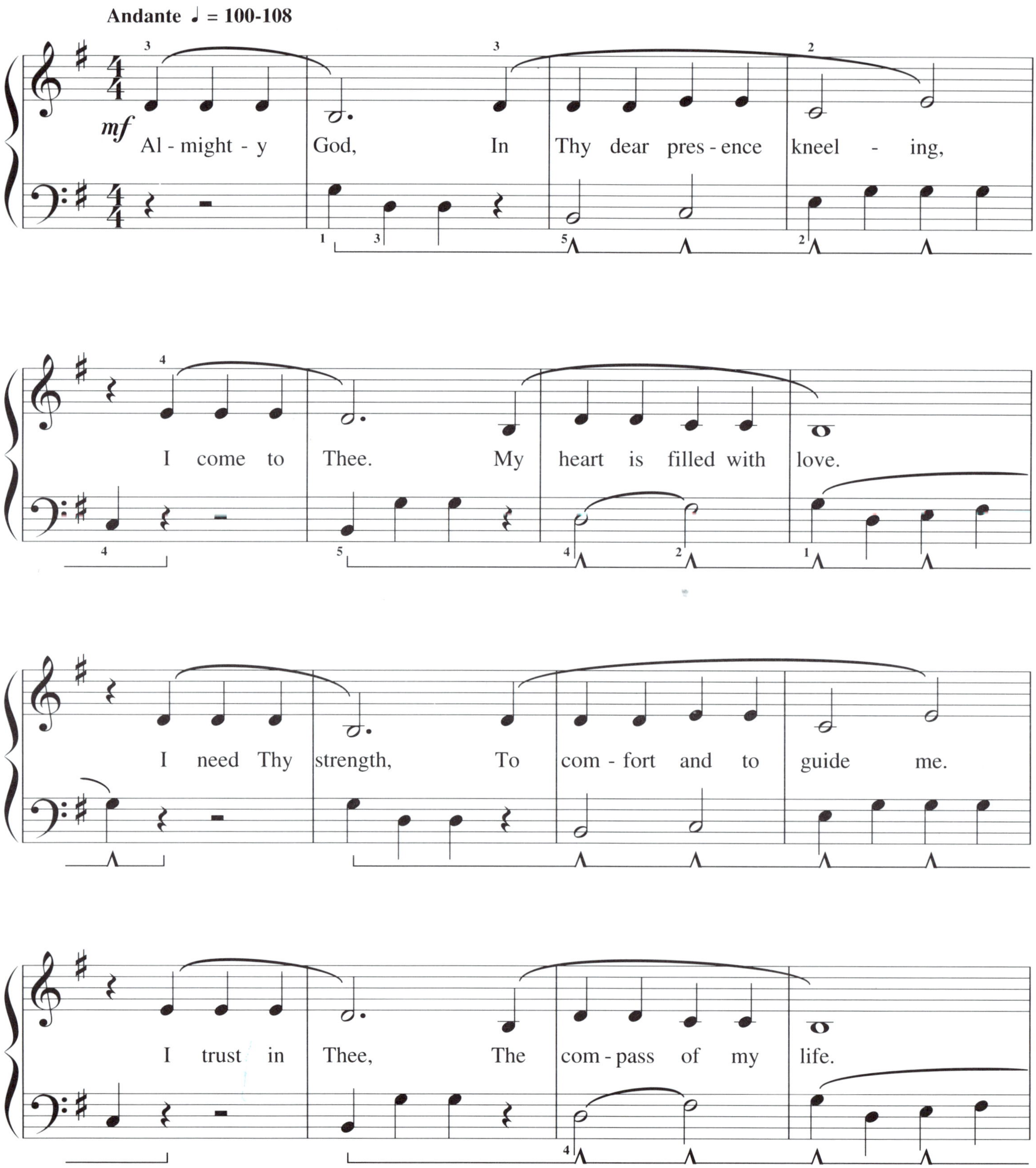

I sing to Thee A song of praise and joy.
How great Thou art. How great Thou art.
Thy peace and love Live on e - ter - nal - ly.
How great Thou art. How great Thou art.
rit.

WOODLAND MELODY

Original Solo by
Carol Foster Masson

Espressivo ♩ **= 104-116**

f
mp

ABOMINABLE SNOWMAN

Original Solo by
Lillian K. Durocher

Misterioso ♩ = **144-168**

NOTE: There are many reported "Abominable Snowmen," and all are virtually a mystery in our world of scientific achievements. Many of these legendary creatures have been said to be seen on all the continents. The most famous one is the "Yeti," which, according to legend, exists in the region of Mt. Everest of the Himalayas in Nepal. "Yeti" is the name that the Shirpas, natives of the region, have given him.

Take Me Out To The Ball Game

Albert Von Tilzer
arr. by John W. Schaum

Vivace ♩ = 176-184

root, root, root for the home team, If
they don't win it's a shame. For it's
one, two, three strikes, you're out at the
old ball game.
cresc.
ff

AMERICA The BEAUTIFUL

Words by Katherine Lee Bates

Music by Samuel A. Ward
arr. by John W. Schaum

broth - er-hood From sea to shin - ing sea. 2. O beau - ti-ful for
basso marcato
pil - grim feet, Whose stern, im - pas - sion'd stress, A thor - ough-fare of
free - dom beat, A - cross the wil - der - ness. A -
mer - i-ca, A - mer - i-ca, God mend thine ev - 'ry flaw, Con -
firm thy soul in self con-trol, Thy lib - er - ty in law.

PACHELBEL'S CANON

Johann Pachelbel
arr. by Wesley Schaum

mf
p
mp
f
mp
f
mp
mf
ff
rit.

PARADE of The TOY SOLDIERS

Leon Jessel
arr. by Wesley Schaum

f
basso marcato
melodia marcato
mp
pp
poco a poco cresc.
mf
basso
marcato

melodia marcato
mf
f
p
cresc.
f